FEMALE PART OF THE FLOWER
MALE PART OF THE FLOWER
STIGMA
PISTIL-STYLE
OVARY
RECEPTICLE
STALK
ANTHER
FILAMENT
STAMEN
PETAL
SEPAL
What's up?
ons
info
oesn't
... It isn't
don't know
to think...
But I do want to understand it all better, and maybe I will understand myself better if I do.
Yeh I felt the same. I was really confused at first and didn't know where to start. So I did what I always do when I don't understand a word - I look it up in the dictionary. Let's look!
Sex
The state of being male or female
Male
1. Being a man or a boy.
Female
1. Being a woman or a girl.

...That helped a bit but didn't explain everything. So I asked Hannah - she is well into this; science, biology, humans etc - this is her special interest. She explained it really clearly to me, Why dont you ask her?
Yeah! Daler's right! She knows her stuff - you should definitely ask her!
I don't know her that well... But if you both don't think she would mind... Then I will!
So lots of people have questions about sex and gender. Especially when there are groups of people who describe these things differently. But! Most people agree on the basics:
XX
XY
A person's sex is their male or female body.
Humans are mammals, mammals have two sexes.
Females have XX chromosomes and are the sex that produce large gametes. Women and girls have primary sex characteristics:- uterus, ovaries, vagina, vulva. Women have secondary sex characteristics:- breasts, pubic hair, body hair and have a monthly period.
Awesome! So this is pretty clear, and what we are learning in biology class. But people have been talking about other stuff...
Like hormones? What about all that?
Yes! Hormones are so important, they regulate our monthly cycle & give us periods but boys have hormones too.

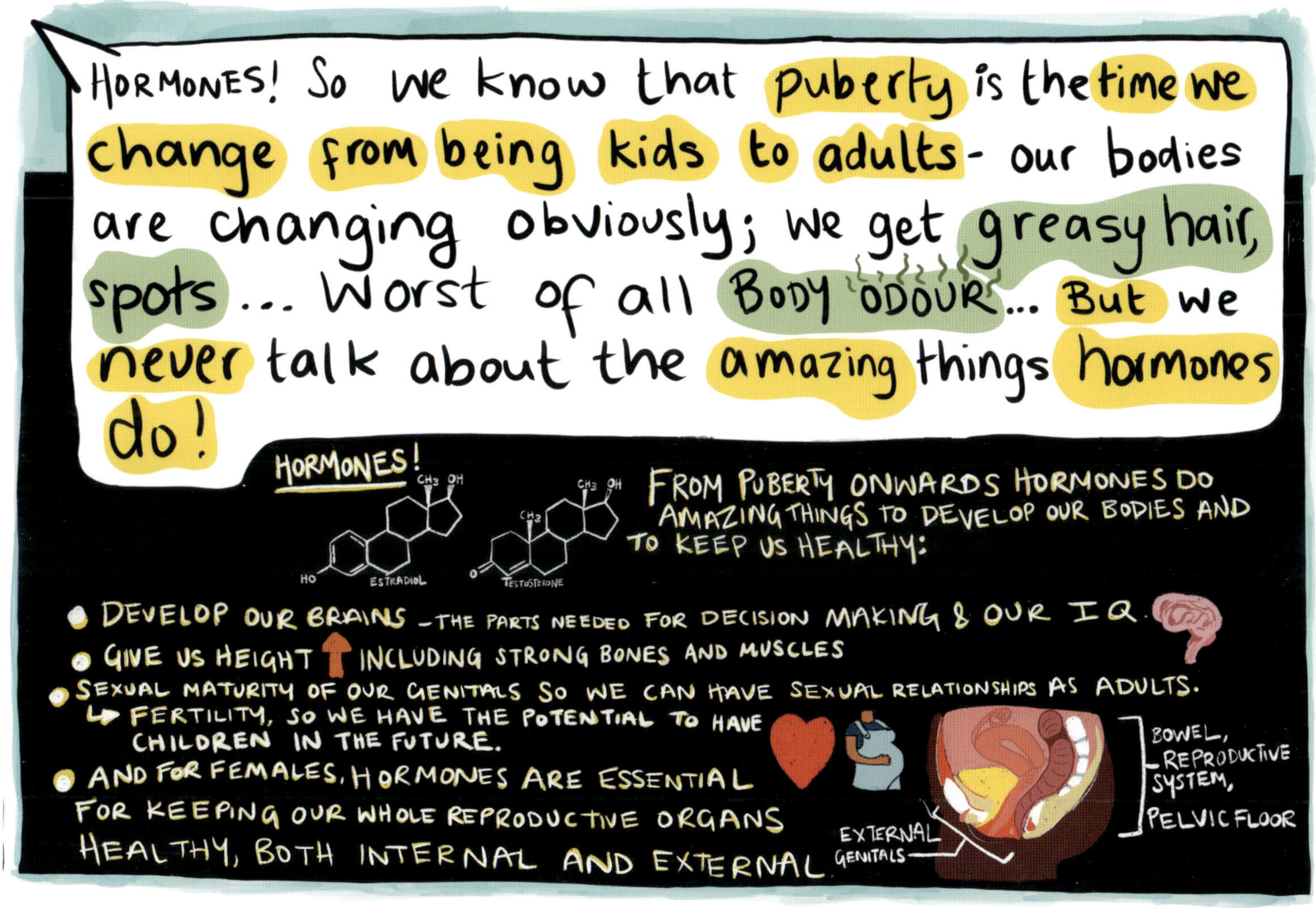
HORMONES! So we know that puberty is the time we change from being kids to adults - our bodies are changing obviously; we get greasy hair, spots ... Worst of all BODY ODOUR... But we never talk about the amazing things hormones do!
HORMONES!
CH3 OH
HO
ESTRADIOL
CH3 OH
CH3
O
TESTOSTERONE
FROM PUBERTY ONWARDS HORMONES DO AMAZING THINGS TO DEVELOP OUR BODIES AND TO KEEP US HEALTHY:
DEVELOP OUR BRAINS - THE PARTS NEEDED FOR DECISION MAKING & OUR IQ.
GIVE US HEIGHT INCLUDING STRONG BONES AND MUSCLES
SEXUAL MATURITY OF OUR GENITALS SO WE CAN HAVE SEXUAL RELATIONSHIPS AS ADULTS.
FERTILITY, SO WE HAVE THE POTENTIAL TO HAVE CHILDREN IN THE FUTURE.
AND FOR FEMALES, HORMONES ARE ESSENTIAL FOR KEEPING OUR WHOLE REPRODUCTIVE ORGANS HEALTHY, BOTH INTERNAL AND EXTERNAL.
BOWEL,
REPRODUCTIVE SYSTEM,
PELVIC FLOOR
EXTERNAL GENITALS

Hormones keep our reproductive organs healthy?!
It says here that not only do sex hormones make us fertile, they also keep our vulva and urethra healthy. Not only that, sex hormones in girls & boys make our skin, bones, heart & immune system strong and healthy!
Without these hormones we would be in pain... So balanced female hormones enable us to run, swim, sit comfortably and be active!
I never knew all of this!
Yeh the endocrine (hormone) system is fascinating stuff!
The Menstrual Cycle
Menstruation
Proliferative Phase
Ovulation
Secretory Phase
Growing follicle
THE TIME A WOMAN CAN GET PREGNANT IS 5-6 DAYS BEFORE OVULATION & 12-24 HOURS AFTER
THE EGG TRAVELS
From the ovary to the fallopian tube, the uterus then out of the body
'FOLLICULAR PHASE'
'LUTEAL PHASE'
Hormone levels rise & fall
Last months egg & lining are shed by the body
DAY 1
PERIOD
DAY 7
DAY 14 IS OVULATION
DAY 21
DAY 28

Back to sex though - we didn't finish talking about boys & men!
We also have very specific experiences as boys during puberty - like when our voices started breaking...
Males are the sex that produce small gametes and have xy chromosomes. Men & boys have primary sex characteristics:- penis, testicles, prostate, seminal vesicles & vas deferens.
Men have secondary sex characteristics such as pubic hair, facial & body hair, & an adam's apple.
Chromosomes!!!
female
male
This is the small gamete - the sperm, approximately 1/16 th of the size of this large gamete, the egg!
The large gamete the egg

A small number of people (0.02–0.2%) are born with differences of sex development, sometimes referred to as a DSD or intersex variation. This may be observed at birth as the baby's genitals may look different to what is typically expected for boys or girls, or may only be noticed at puberty when development doesn't happen as expected.

There are over 40 different conditions that can lead to DSD, including differences in chromosomes and response to hormones – and can sometimes be associated with medical complications. Most people with a DSD are observed male or female, just like everyone else. An intersex identity may be really important for some people born with a DSD, whereas others may prefer only to use condition specific terminology, not referred to as intersex. Young people with DSD's need support & good friends as well as sensitive medical care. DSD's are about congenital physical differences of the reproductive system, not gender.

If your friend has a DSD, listen to them & be supportive.

...Okay... So erm... what about sexual orientation? Ugh I feel so shy!!! So yeah?
Eww-nope not interested!
SAME LOL
I'm also shy!!!
Yeah this is pretty straightforward! I am happy to talk about it with you!
This is about who you are attracted to - if you want to date men or women, or men & women.
SEXUAL ORIENTATION
♀♥♀ = Lesbian, female & same sex attracted
♂♥♂ = Gay, male & same sex attracted
♀♥♂ = Heterosexual, opposite sex attracted
You ♥ ♀ or ♂ = Bisexual, attracted to the same & opposite sex to you!
P.S - SEXUAL ORIENTATION IS JUST WHO YOU ARE ATTRACTED TO - NOT A TYPE OF PERSONALITY - ALL ARE FINE & NORMAL
I think I might be bisexual because I am same sex and opposite sex attracted. But there is no pressure to decide your orientation any time soon. Whenever you're ready!
Oh good!
Yeah! You might not feel that attraction yet, or you might decide you are happy to be single! And if you do decide to date you can just hold hands or kiss. There's plenty of time for sex in the future - we aren't even 16 yet!
16?
Yeah! That's the legal age of consent!

But what about 'gender'? What even is it? Is it like your personality or something?
Yeah 'gender' is really confusing!
SNAP!
Haha!
So we often think that gender = sex, like when we talk about 'gender equality' or when we fill out forms & it says gender: male ☐ female ☐... But that's not it...
... Don't need no labels nah just wanna be me You can do it your way But I'M GONNA BE FREE!
Shall we check the dictionary again? It is something about 'gender roles'...

Gender noun
/ˈdʒɛndər/
1. The fact of being male or female when in reference to social & cultural differences, not differences in biology.
• gender roles
• issues of race, class and gender.
• traditional concepts of gender
2. The grammatical arrangement of nouns, pronouns and adjectives to masculine, feminine & neuter in some languages.
Social & cultural! So these are the ideas & traditions pushed onto girls & boys, women & men! Gender ROLES! These are basically old fashioned stereotypes that say boys MUST behave one way, and girls MUST behave another!
This is what sexism means, especially towards women & girls who had to fight for equal rights - my mum & grandmother did loads of protests!
Ashley that is SO COOL!!!

But gender splits human traits, hobbies, even JOBS into two - it says "this is for boys only" and "this is for girls only." What if I like 'boy things'?! Or Billy likes 'girl things'?!
YEAH! I like baking cakes. I'm a BOY. Why is baking labelled a 'girl thing'?!
Yeah Hannah you do climbing and I play footie AND do ballet classes! Girls CAN love BOTH! Both make me happy in different ways - I'm STILL a girl!
YEP. It is a really old fashioned idea, gender. I especially don't like the idea of 'boy personalities' or 'girl personalities'.

I made notes - it's like this. It helps me to visualise.
Yes the first one! My personality is unique to ME.
I know right! I have lived here AND in Amman; having two cultures makes me feel unique!
Sexist stereotypes are bad like racist stereotypes are bad!
Yuuuuup 100% agree!
This is how humans are:
KEY
= PERSONALITY
= SEX, MALE OR FEMALE
Human personality = infinite types!
You are UNIQUE! There is no one else like you! And no one else has lived your life!
Biological sex, female or male
PERSONALITY = YOUR THOUGHTS, FEELINGS, LIKES AND DISLIKES.
Our bodies + our personality = Who we are - they are not separate; we experience our feelings and thoughts in our bodies!
Female or Male
FREE ME!
CHAINS
Break my chains! I am just ME!
But this is what the social construct (made up idea) of gender is:
GENDER - The idea that your sex controls your personality...
AKA STEREOTYPES!!!
ie. "only boys are clever"
"only girls are caring"
NOPE.

What's wrong? Are you okay?
Oh Jordan please tell us we care about you!
Ever since I was a little girl I didn't fit in with other girls. I didn't like 'girl things'. I was always given toys I didn't like, & clothes I didn't like - & no one was trying to be mean - but they all presumed that because I am a girl, girls = 'girly'. It made me feel like I was a rubbish girl & that I was the problem. That there was something wrong with me. This is the first time I have ever felt that I am a normal girl, & the problem is not me, but outside of me - the problem is old fashioned sexist ideas... And I just feel so... RELIEVED! In fact, I want to learn more!
You're not alone Jordan, I felt like that too - & Billy & Ashley!

After spending ALL lunch break reading...
So I read some history & it helped me to understand! So over time Society (people) created rules of what people could or couldn't do.
In prehistory - way before farming, the rules were very different! Women were also warriors & hunters! We know because they found weapons in women's graves!
Yes! And sexist stereotypes appear to have been made later. Over time, society made many rules, especially for women & men. They were strict, & people were very unhappy.
These rules became the old fashioned view that our sex (being male or female) put us into a box:
BOYS MUST BE LIKE THIS!
GIRLS MUST BE LIKE THIS
SEXIST STEREOTYPES IN TWO BOXES.
But then women said "hang on, this is no good for us! say no to sexism!"
We left the box! Now to remove the sexist chains in law!

Culture was changing! Laws were made to challenge sexism - like equal pay for women! There was still a long way to go, but things started to improve! Men and women enjoyed awesome clothes & music! It was the 1970's & boys & girls could step out of the blue or pink box! Long hair, short hair - all grooovy! But some people did not like this change. They were so used to living in a box that they couldn't imagine living outside of one! They thought their personality was a box. So they created lots of new boxes, with colourful flags and labels. And encouraged people to go back into boxes. And this is where we are today...
♀WOMEN'S LIBERATION!♀
I don't know who I am because I was in a box for so long
SEXIST STEREOTYPES IN LOTS OF BOXES
I know! Lets make new boxes, let's tell everyone to go back into boxes, but instead of two there are loads!

But if you live in a box, can you ever grow? Won't you always be stuck? What would it be like to live outside of these boxes?! What if boxes were for things not people? Can we live differently and be free? Wouldn't that be liberating?!
What if... we didn't go back into a box?
?
I'm off on an adventure of self discovery!
Don't want you anymore! Sexism can go in the bin!
A new wave for liberation!
Yes! That's such a great way of putting it!

What a day! School's over..
Ready to chill! Sure you folks don't want to come skating with us tonight?
Not so well today so gonna give it a miss- we also need to do some band practice for the gig! But thanks anyway! See ya!
See you all tommorrow!
Daler, you want me and Jordan to pick up some ice cream on the way over?
Yeah cool! Thanks!

It's so cool to meet another girl who is more like me! But I love the others too!
Wow what a day! I learned so much! I'm so happy that we are friends!
How do you feel now?
Haha! Well I have one final question... You know hormones develop our brains?
Yeah...
When does that stop? I mean, how old do we have to be until our brains are fully... Developed?!
I read at age 25! The prefrontal cortex is developed by age 25.
Whaaat?! Hahahaha NOWAY! Well I guess that means more time for FUN STUFF!!!
Exactly!

Just moved to a new school
NAME: Jordan
AGE: 15
HOBBIES:
playing the drums.
Comics.
Gaming.
INTERESTS:
Everything about music & art.
FAVOURITE FOOD:
Sushi or falafel wraps.
NAME: Daler
AGE: 15 nearly 16
HOBBIES:
Plays the guitar & the piano.
INTERESTS:
Music, music, music!
Dreams of travelling
FAVOURITE FOOD:
Always PIZZAAA
Jordan's first new friend & bandmate!

Together they plan the BEST adventures
NAME: Ashley
AGE: 15
HOBBIES:
Hiking.
Reading.
Skateboarding.
INTERESTS:
The environment & wildlife & hip hop.
FAVOURITE FOOD:
Vegan curry & dhosa & bhaji.
NAME: Hannah
HOBBIES:
Climbing
Rockpooling
AGE: 15
INTERESTS:
Biology, nature & evolution.
Her tortoise Tommy.
FAVOURITE FOOD:
Veggie tempura & ice cream.
ADHD
Both neurodiverse!
Autistic

Both love sport
NAME: Bilal aka 'Billy'
AGE: 15
HOBBIES:
Baking.
Roller skating.
Football.
INTERESTS:
Films - Scifi, thrillers & comedies. History.
FAVOURITE FOOD:
Tacos & ALL the cakes!!!
NAME: Jessica
AGE: 14
HOBBIES:
Ballet.
Football.
Roller skating
INTERESTS:
Films - especially musicals & Scifi. Her dog Elphaba
FAVOURITE FOOD:
Ramen & Billy's cakes!
Started their own film club!